AF455211

#1 Hit

Prompts that will make your imagination soar through a wonder of creative writing!
Simply the most needed book to begin a fictional-story for everyone to read or a personal (private) journal for your own counseling and entertainment.

The Easy Way

By: Georgina Jones

Creative Writing
~
The Easy Way

By: Georgina Jones

Prompts that will make your imagination soar through a wonder of creative writing!

www.georginajones.net
www.lulu.com
ISBN 978-1-257-08921-5

Creative Writing ~ The Easy Way

Writing makes things happen!

Do you remember the first time you ever wrote a story on your own? If you do, you probably remember what a thrill it was to see your ideas on paper. When you are the writer, ***you*** are the person who makes things happen.

When you write, you can do all sorts of things that aren't possible in real life. You can jump the tallest mountain on a bicycle. You can swim to the deepest of seas to find expensive treasures. You can even put your enemy's out on the plant Mars.

Writing can help you do other things, too. You can write your inter-most thoughts in a private journal. You can share your joys, disappointments, and feelings with your best friend, no matter where they may live. You can even ask for a raise at work through writing. Anything that you may feel or imagine you can put into words.

This book will help you write about whatever is important to you. It will also help you start to write your own book or books.

Before you can write, you need something to write about. You can use the starter prompts provided in this book. You can use your imagine, you can use your own life, or even do research to begin a how-to-do it book. It all depends on what you want to write about. But you need to organize your ideas so that they make sense.

In this book you will be starting to write a lot of different stories. Some of them will be stories you make up from your imagination. Some will be stories that are based on your own experiences.

- When you write stories from you own experience, you should already have a plot. You job will be to make the story interesting. Use will need to use a lot of descriptions, action, and dialogue. This will help your reader feel what you felt.

- When you write stories using your imagination, you get a bravura chance to make up what happened. Who are the people? What do they look like? How are they acting? Make sure to put in convincing details that will keep your reader interested and imagining what you are writing.

How do writers think of details that are convincing? One way to find out is to read the kinds of stories you plan on writing. As you are reading, look at the kinds of details that author uses. Remember to examine and use the same kind of details in your own writing.

Imagination Rocks!

1 Horn 4 Arm Cyclops

Elijah Erwood
9 yrs. old

Organizing your Stories

When coming up with ideas, don't let anything stop the flow of your thoughts. You need to mentally see the words flowing. Think of as many ideas as you can. Let one idea lead to another and another. Just make sure you write down all of those ideas.

Once you have gathered your ideas decide which ones you want to keep. Then organize your ideas. There are many different ways to organize ideas. And don't forget that you will always need a beginning, a middle, and an end.

To organize a Fictional Narrative story, use the following as a guideline.

BEGINNING

- Introduce the characters.
- Describe the setting.
- Hint at the trouble.

MIDDLE

- Show the characters talking and doing things.
- Show the characters' problems.
- Show the characters' feelings.
- Hint at how the problems will be solved.

END

- Show how the problems are solved.
- Show the characters' feelings.
- Show how the characters are changed.

To organize a Personal Narrative story, use the following as a guideline.

BEGINNING

- Tell the main idea.
- Introduce the characters.
- Describe the setting.

MIDDLE

- Tell the events in order.
- Show the characters talking and doing things.
- Give many details.
- Show the characters' feelings.

END

- Tell how the story ends.
- Tell your feelings about the ending.
- Tell why the ideas and events in the story are important to you.

Here is another way to help you get ideas; it's called a Graphic Organizer.

Let's say you read a story about a pet. First draw a picture of the pet, either on paper or simply in your head. Now you want to write a story or a poem about this pet. Use the graph below to help you get started.

PET'S NAME

What kind of animal is this pet?

Whose pet is it?

What is special about this pet?

What does this pet like to do?

How do you feel about this pet?

Is there anything else you want to say about this pet?

Does this pet's name fit?
Why or why not?

This is Your Voice

There are all kinds of ways to put your ideas on paper. What if you want to tell about a book you just read? You could describe it in a letter to your pen pal, you could write a report about the book for your teacher at school, or you could write about it in your private journal. Describing this book in three different ways will help you be able to pick the best way for you to write and say what you want.

Anything you can say out loud or to yourself can be put on paper. In many ways, writing and talking are the same. If you try to write the same way you talk, writing can be easy. If you try to sound like someone else instead of yourself, your writing won't be as interesting to your readers.

You have only one voice so let it speak; although you *can* use it in many different ways. You can use it to make a serious speech to your class. You can use it to tell a silly joke. In both cases, your voice would probably sound different. The same is true when you write.

Who is the Reader of what you will be writing?

Sometimes the way you say things depends on whom you're saying them to. You wouldn't talk to a police officer the same way you would talk to your best friend.

When you are writing to your friend you will find yourself using a different language than if you were writing to your friend's parents. The letter to your friend will be more casual and it might even contain slang. But the letter to your friend's parents will be more formal.

Knowing what kind of language to use is a big part of writing. More formal language is used for adults and people you don't know well. More casual language and slang are used for close family, good friends, or for writing in a journal. Stories often use casual language, when reports for school or work are needed you should use formal language.

Casual everyday language is easy to write. It is written just as you speak it, while formal language can be a little bit harder to write.

Pay very good attention to details.

Sometimes we write as if we are trying to get the job over quickly. We use general words that give very little information. Take this sentence for example:

The girl played ball.

What or who is the girl? What kind of ball was she playing? Was she good at playing ball? What if we said:

The cute red headed little girl, Karen, played T-ball just as well as the boys did.

Now we have a much better picture of what you are trying to say.

Variety is better than boring

A single idea can be expressed in many different ways. Imagine you are writing a story about a boat being shipped wreck on a deserted island. Think about how you could tell your readers the following ideas about the island.

- The island was covered with trees.
- The island was hot and wet.
- The island was enormous.

You could write these three ideas in many different ways.

- Weeping trees with fruit covered the hot, wet, enormous island.
- The island was hot, wet, and it was covered with weeping trees that bloom fruit.
- Covering the enormous island was weeping fruit trees.

You'll have more fun writing when you use different kinds of sentences and your readers will have more fun reading it too.

Topic and staying on top of it

When you are writing a story, sometimes your thoughts can get off track. Getting off track may be fine when you are talking, but it doesn't work very well in writing. When you write you should stick to the main topic. The topic is the main idea you are talking about. Everything you write should help your readers understand the topic. To help you stay on topic, you could use the graph below.

TOPIC (Main Idea):			
SUPPORTING IDEAS	1. ______ ______ ______ 2. ______ ______ ______	SUPPORTING IDEAS	3. ______ ______ ______ 4. ______ ______ ______

Connecting Your Sentences and Ideas

Good writers place their sentences in logical order. It is very important to learn how to connect your sentences. You can improve the organization of your writing and ideas, as the result of doing these things is called coherence.

Here are a few examples of words and phrases that can help improve your writing.

- Add more facts: also, again, another, next, to begin with
- Compare something similar: also, as, in the same way
- Contrast something: but, although, even though, however, instead, yet
- Identify a place: above, below, beyond, nearby, under, there
- Emphasize something: in fact, indeed, of course, certainly
- Repeat an important point: all of this means, in other words, to conclude
- Give an example: for example, in particular, a few of these are
- Give the result of something: for this reason, obviously, so, therefore
- Identify the time: after, as soon as, before, finally, later, now, until, when, while, afterward

Editing and Revising

You've gathered your ideas and organized them well. You've put them down on paper. Now what, right?

After great writers have written what they want to say, they go back and edit their work. Editing your work will help you polish your writing and make it the best it can be.

You can learn to polish your own writing in much the same way an editor can. After you finish putting your ideas down on paper, go back to the beginning. Read what you have written. This time pretend that you are an editor instead of a writer. Pretend you are reading the ideas for the very first time. Below are some qualities that you should look for when you edit:

- Writing stays focused on topic.
- Writing uses details to support topic.
- Writing is well organized and complete. It has a beginning, a middle, and an end.
- Use different kinds of words. Do not use the same words over and over.
- Use different kinds of sentences in writing.
- Choose words that make your meaning clear.
- Spell the words correctly.
- Handwriting is easy for others to read.
- Sentences and proper names begin with a capital letter.
- Sentences end with a period, exclamation mark, or a question mark.

Proofreader Marks

Editor's and proofreader also use symbols to show where problems lie. Here are a few of their marks, so you can use them while editing your own writing.

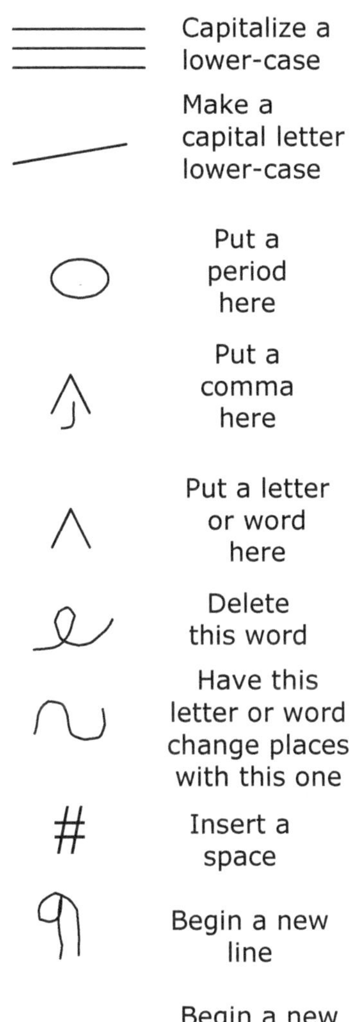

As you read through your writing, you may find that you need to make a few changes to your work. The best writers often make many changes as they work. It is okay to erase or cross out as long as your changes are done neatly.

Your readers won't know whether they like your writing if they are unable to read it. Your final copy should be neat enough for others to read it easily. You may want to write in print, cursive, or use a printer to print out your work.

Writing Prompts

Think about the differences between old dances and new ones. Try to recall an old dance you have seen on TV or in movies, like "Milking the Cow". Then think about a new dance you have seen or done yourself, like "The Electric Slide".
Write a paragraph describing the similarities and differences between the two. Provide enough details to make the differences stand out and be clear to your readers.

Imagine you are a scientist working on a satellite that will be sent deep into space! You want to enclose a message on the satellite for any intelligent life form that might intercept it.
Write your message and think about the most important things about our plant Earth and its people. Put in as much details as you think is necessary for those other life forms to learn from and about us.

Pick out a picture of yourself and write a biography paragraph on this picture. Use the boxes below to organize your ideas. List what is important to you. Include people, things, and ideas. List the feelings you want to convey about yourself to someone looking at your picture. Use your notes to describe how you will depict the event, ideas, and feeling in your picture.

This picture holds a dear event in my life	What is in the picture that is so important to me	Feelings I want to convey about this picture

Think about your five senses (sight, hearing, smell, touch, and taste). Which one do you appreciate the most? Which one would you miss the most? Pretend you have lost one sense. Write a letter to your best friend describing how and why you lost that precious sense. Tell how the loss of this sense is involved in the making of your world as of now.

Christmas is a special day for a lot of people. What is your favorite holiday? What is so special about it? Why do you like that certain holiday the most? Do you eat any special foods? Is there a special place or a special person on which you spend it with?
Write a story using only 10 lines to tell about your special holiday.

Environmental issues have concerned environmentalist and others about our earth. What are four ways that people are harming the Earth? Write an expressive article for a magazine that tells about one practice that is harming our environment. In your article be sure to describe this practice and why you believe they are the ones harming our environment. What are they doing? How are they wrenching our environment? How can they do their job without harming the environment? Explain the above questions so your readers will understand what is going on in their practice.

Imagine that a housing developer wants to build apartments in an area that archaeologist strongly believe is filled with objects from the Colonial times. The apartments are desperately needed in your area, but the construction might destroy valuable artifacts.
Write a paragraph in which you try to persuade others, in your opinion, whether the excavating should proceed or be delayed. First state your opinion, and then give precise facts that back you up.

After a major volcano has erupted, reporters are sent out to the scene to find out what has happened. They try to interview people who have lived through this eruption. They do this to get the most accurate information about the sequence of events. Imagine you are one of the reporters reporting on this volcano. Write five questions that you will ask a person you are interviewing. Then in 3rd person, answer these questions as specifically as you can. This will convey a "Who's Who" article.

Is there a daring and adventurous career that you might enjoy doing? Such as racing cars or bikes, climbing mountains to save others, or jumping out of airplanes to deliver food to other countries. Write a paragraph that identifies and discusses this adventurous career. Be sure to include details that describe the challenges that this career might bring upon you or others.

Pretend it is time for you to get your first pet animal. Mom and Dad have taken you to a local shelter that has every animal you could think of. Write a journal page telling about the animal you choose and why it is your favorite. What color is it? Why did you choose this one? How do you plan on taking care of it?

Hansel and Gretel came upon a house in the woods made of candy. This is a house they have only dreamt of. What is your dream home made of? Bricks, ice, hotdogs, paper, etc...? Draw a picture of what it would look like.

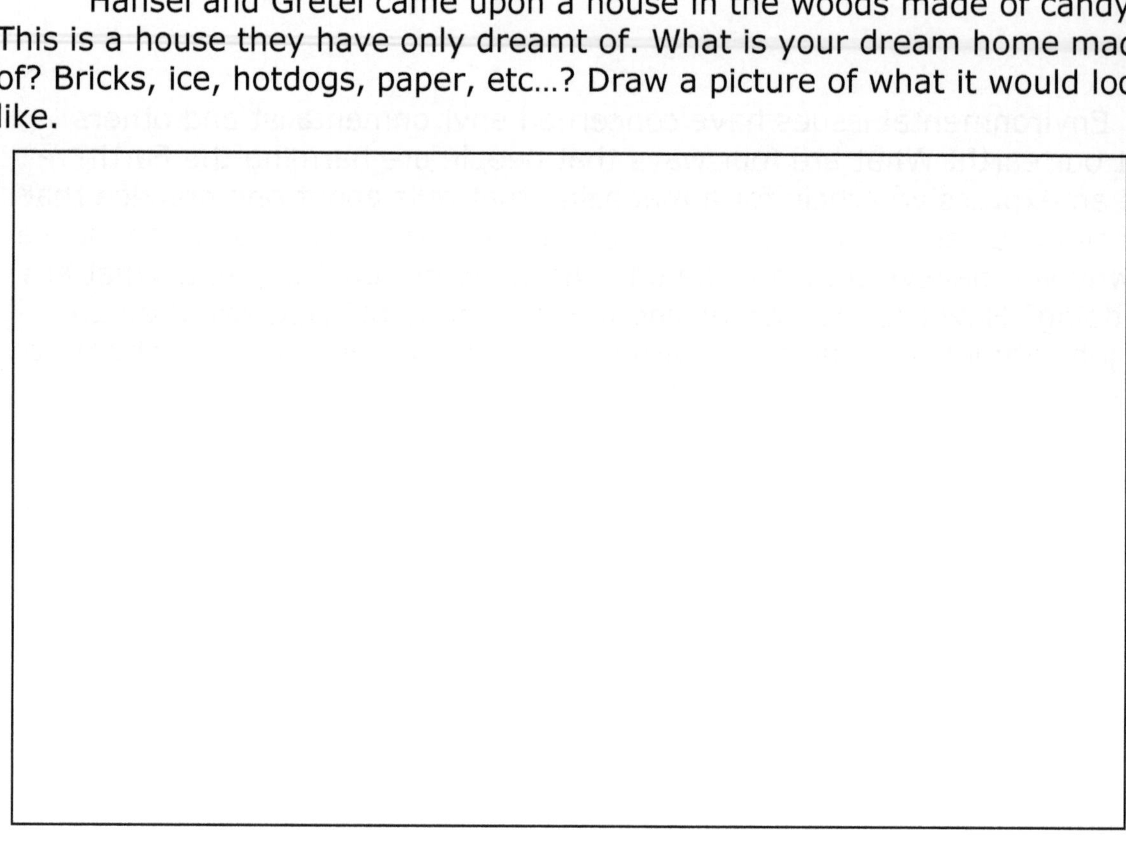

Write a story telling about your dream home. Tell what it is made of, where it would be located, and who would be living in this dream home with you.

Deep-sea diver, Fox McAdams, loves to keep a journal on the things that happen to him while he is underwater. Imagine you are Fox's friend and you are spending the day under the Atlantic Ocean with him. Write at least two journal pages on how you spent the day. What did you see? Did you get hurt? Did you find something valuable underwater? What is Fox like?

Think about what it would be like to be an animal trainer at your local zoo. What animal would you like to work with? Would it be fun or dangerous? Write an article telling about your job as an animal trainer and what it takes to complete your job safely.

Pick an animal that you adore. Do research on this animal. Write a research paper on this animal and it's habit. This will help teach you how to do research and what to write. Do not infuse on the copyright of your research.

Pretend you and your family is appearing on a reality show. Pick one or two funny things about your family and write a TV sitcom. Imagine what will happen during the first episode. Be sure to tell the plot in order of which they come.

A comic book publication has called you to create a new super hero and/or villain for their up-coming annual edition. Imagine what your new super hero or villain will look like. Draw a picture of it, using your mental vision to see the picture in whole. Then draw two more to go with the first one. Under each picture write a comic strip to go along with it.

Halloween poses a night where ghost and goblins appear. Pretend you go to a very old house and the electricity begins to flicker. Could it be a ghost or maybe the works of someone playing a cruel joke on you?

Write 2 pages in your personal journal about your experience in this old scary house. Explain what scared you. Make it believable, so that others will believe it truly happened. Whether it has or not.

Do you have an invention plastered to the sides of your mind? Something no one else has ever thought of? How about the Grabber or bathroom wipes?

Draw your invention on a piece of drawing paper. Under your drawing write a paragraph telling about your invention and how it works. Remember to describe why you invented it. (For a paper in one of my writing classes, I choose and wrote about a Voice Activated (Remoteless) TV. Your imagination is limitless. Go wild.)

Pretend you are skydiving for the very first time. Your heart is thumping, ready to jump from your body, just as you start to jump from the plane.

Write a page in your private journal about your day and experience in skydiving. Give us the thrill of jumping out of a plane. Include how you felt and what you saw.

Are you fat, skinny, blonde, a brunette, an artist or maybe a construction worker? Have you ever been ridiculed for any reason?

Write about your experience in your personal journal, using 1 page only. Explain what the issue was, how you handled it, and how it was resolved.

Imagine what you might look like in twenty years. Describe the way you think you will look. Will you have gray hair or be bald? Will you be as hip as you are now? How about the differences in clothing?

Write a brief story describing how you think your appearance and surroundings have changed for the future.

Which is your favorite appliance? TV, the radio, or the computer?
Write a story using one of the above appliances. Use this appliance as something evil or as the hero in the story. Remember to make it seem real. Make the readers want more.

You are a member of the PTO at your child's school. Suppose you found a way to be eligible to receive free computers. But first, you must convince the other members of the PTO that the computers will benefit the school and students to help aid the learning process.

Write a paragraph explaining some of the ways students would use the computers. Explain ways they will enhance the student's knowledge and why they would benefit the school.

Think about some of the fairy tales that were read to you as a child. Create a fairy tale character of your own. Draw a picture of it so you can get a visual of it, then write a fairy tale to go along with your character.

Imagine what it would be like to live on an uninhabited island; think about the things you use and take for granted everyday. Describe them and how it would be unavailable to you on the island.

In a paragraph, describe what your life would be like on this lonely island. Explain how you would go about getting food, clothing, shelter and other things needed to survive.

The Redwood Forest, Mt. Mitchell, and the Grand Canyon, are only a few of our natural wonders on this earth. Pick a natural earthly wonder that you have been to or would like to go to.

Write a 50-line story about that place. Include the location, atmosphere, and why it is your choice.

Do you know someone who is a member of a helping profession, such as a teacher, doctor, or fireman?

Describe this person in two paragraphs. Explain what that person does and why they do their job? Tell whether you might enjoy this profession for yourself.

Amusement parks are everyone's favorite past time. Roller coasters, The Devils Twin, the swings, or maybe it's the games that draws you near? What is your favorite thing to do in an amusement park?

Write a story, using no more than 500 words, telling about your adventure in an amusement park. Describe what your favorite thing is and how it makes you feel?

Imagine that a magazine has hired you to write about your experiences during a disaster; think of a personal or natural disaster you have experience.

Write an article about this experience. Tell when each event happened and how you and others deal with the emergency and fears associated with this disaster.

Remember your favorite novel or bedtime story. Think about the ending of it and how it kept your attention to the end. Pretend you are the main character in this story.

In your own opinion, write your versions of that ending using you as the character. Remember that this ending needs to hold your reader's attention and interest as much as the beginning does.

Pretend you just got home from a birthday party. Write a 750-word story about this party. Tell who the party was held for and what you did to make the party a success.

You are a newspaper reporter for the greatest newspaper in your state. Something extraordinary has just happened locally and you are the reporter called to write the story.

Write your story on what just happened and where. Remember to tell the how, when, and why it happened.

Think about your favorite TV shows. Imagine you are a judge for this year TV Show Awards.

Write a paragraph that will convince the other judges to vote for your favorite show. What is the show? Why should they vote for it? Give specific reasons to support your opinion.

Hundreds of newspapers reported the onset of Hurricane Hugo. People all over the world wants to know what went on.

Most of the newspapers answered the basic questions in the first paragraph:

- What happened?
- Who was affected?
- When did it happen?
- Why did it happen?
- Where did it happen?

These are the five W's that are the core of the first paragraph in a good newspaper report.

Chose an event and write a story that can serve as a first paragraph in a newspaper report about this particular event.

WEATHER CHRONICLES

____
Date

____

____

____

____

____

____

____

Think about the different kinds of weather: rain, snow, sleet, overcast, or sun. Which weather do you like the best? Be a weather reporter on your local TV network.

Write a 15-line weather broadcast, using your favorite weather as your broadcast line. Make your readers believe that today's broadcast is really happening outside.

Logbooks of entries from travelers tell about events in the sequence in which they actually happen. Imagine that you and a classmate are the astronauts in the space capsule.

Write a logbook entry that describes an exciting moment during your flight. In sequential order, tell what you experienced and how you felt about it.

You volunteer for the local newspaper to take a ride in a hot air balloon. Suddenly a few events happen leaving everyone frightened, but safe.

Write an article describing your flight and the adventures you had before landing the balloon. Think about the events that makes your story exciting.

A common communication device such as a telephone or a computer is used in almost every home. But one day you come across someone, who has never heard of either one, much less used it.

Write a paragraph explaining what it is used for. Then give step by step directions on how to use it.

Peter wants to be a doctor when he grows up. What do you want to be when you grow up: a policeman, a truck driver, culinary cook, or maybe even a actor?

Write a paragraph telling what you want to be and why you want to do that particular job. Explain some of the special training you need in order to have this dream job.

You just returned home from visiting your great Aunt. She is an old woman who lives deep in the mountains. She lives alone and survives by living of the earth and olden ways.

Write a story about your adventure with her. Be sure to describe your great Aunt, her surroundings and how she lives. How long did you visit her? Did you get along with each other? Did you help her gather food, supplies?

School bands like to play different kinds of music. What kind of music do you like? Is it soft and slow, or hard and loud?

Write a paragraph about your favorite kind of music. Tell what kind of music you like and what it is that you like about it. Also tell why you prefer it to any other music.

If you could be an animal that lives free out in the wild, which one would you be? Draw a picture of this animal.

Next write a journal page describing your day as this animal. Remember to add the exciting adventures you went on that day.

Pretend you just won a trip all expenses paid, to anywhere in the world. Where would you go? Who would you take with you? What would you do?

Write a story describing your well needed free dream trip, using the beginning line below.

"My dream trip to __________________ left my heart at peace once I got there. I got to __________________..."

Its vacation time; you and your best friend have decided to take a sailboat out to an uncharted island, just South of your own native island. Just as you arrive on the island a huge storm appears. The sailboat is washed away in a swill, while you are out looking for shelter.

Write a story telling about your adventure. Did you make a signal fire? What are you eating? Is there any one else on the island? Any animals? Is there a chance of getting off this island or maybe survival on the island?

When a fair comes to town it puts up ads to get the local communities to come see their show. Each ad describes the acts and performers. Imagine that this is your fair.

Write your own ad, telling about your different kinds of acts, performers, and animals. Be sure to add why your circus is the best and why people should buy a ticket to come and see it for themselves.

Circus

Come one, come all!

To the greatest circus around!

You will see:

Your pen pal from another country will be celebrating a birthday soon. Think about how we celebrate birthdays here at home.

Write a letter to your pen pal describing how you celebrate your birthday. Don't forget to wish them a happy birthday as well.

Date ____________________

Happy Birthday Pen Pal!

Dear ________________________,

____

____

____

____

____

____

Bird watching is a calm way to spend your afternoon. How is it that you spend a relaxing evening?

Write two journal pages describing your relaxing evening.

Take your journal to a place and sit where you can watch people. You might choose the airport lobby, a park bench, a bus stop, or playground. Watch one certain person or thing closely. Observe everything about him or her carefully.

Write a journal page of 4 pages. Start with your observations. Be very descriptive as you can to the details or your object. Move on to writing about your quite time and what you observed.

You recently got a job as a cartoon creator. You have been asked to create a new character for an upcoming movie. Draw a picture of your character in the box below.

Write a short story about your character. Be sure to tell about the features of your character. Cartoons are supposed to be funny, so liven up your character by telling what it is? What it looks like? It's name and where it came from?

This story exercise is in two parts. To do this prompt; give us all of the what's, when's, why's, where's, and how's.

First: Write a story describing how you truly spent your 21st birthday.

Secondly: Write a story describing how you would have loved to spend your 21st birthday.

Reread each story. Which one do you like best? Take that story and build a life for it.

In the world of make believe, we can be anyone or anything we want to be. Donna believes that she is a dragon slayer. Tim wants to be a race car driver. What is it that you want to be?

Tell us in 1000-words, what you want to be and why?

Old Mr. Mitchell from down the street, is having problems with raccoons getting into his trashcans at nighttime. You have an idea of how to get rid of them.

Write a story using no more than 1500-words, describing your idea and how you think the raccoons will react to it.

You and your Grandmother have just canned some fresh vegetables from your Grandparents garden. You entered some of the canned tomatoes in the contest at the local fair. You won first prize. The only problem is that you entered the wrong category. You didn't tell anyone that Grandmother helped you.

Write a story of 750-words, describing how you solve this problem.

You are walking down the street and see an injured animal. Do you walk over to the animal or turn and quickly walk a way? Do you help the animal or poke a stick at it?

Write in your personal journal describing your walk down the street and the decision that you made upon the animal.

Imagine that you are going to meet the President. The publication you work for will pay great money for this article.

Write five questions you plan on asking the President and the answers you think he will give you. Using these questions and answers, write an article about him and the interview.

Tonight is the night your daughter goes to the Nationals from the Northwest School District Spelling Bee. You are very proud of her. She can spell words you haven't even heard of.

Write two journal pages to tell about that night at the Spelling Bee. You, as the parent, need to tell how this made you feel? Describe your nervousness and happiness you felt as she came in second.

Imagine being in a mini submarine that can maneuver anywhere in the ocean, even to the lowest bottom. You have your journal with you.

Write three journal pages about your experiences on the ocean floor and what kinds of animals you see.

Pick an item from around the room. Draw your impression of that item.

Now write below your picture about this item. What it the item? How is it used? Where did it come from? Be sure to include lots of details.

Pretend you are back in school and have a project that you've been working on with another person.

Write a paragraph to tell about your project and how you worked as a team. Describe the things that you did to make this project successful.

Find three pictures of your favorite vacation spot. Flyers to these areas are very resourceful.

Write a paragraph of five lines about each picture. Then write a finishing paragraph summarizing all three pictures.

Miss. Amy makes everyone clean their area up in the art room ten minutes before it is time to go. But Mrs. Vickie makes us do it twenty minutes early, then we have to sit quietly until the bell rings. Which teacher do you side with? What would you say to the opposing teacher? Would you get the class involved?

Write a letter to the principle about the complaint. Tell the teacher why you stand behind them?

After finishing your favorite novel, you go out to see the movie they made about it. Suppose the ending of the movie is different than the book.

Write three paragraphs telling the differences between each one.

- First, on how the book ended.
- Second, on how the movie ended.
- Thirdly, give your opinion on how it should have ended for both of them.

Pretend you are on your way home from the zoo. What animals did you see? What sounds did you hear? What kind of smells caught your attention?

Write a journal page of no more than three pages about your day trip to the zoo.

Go outside and sit down. Take a look around you. What do you see? What do you hear? What was that noise? Is the sun shining? Are you near a splashing spring?

Write two journal pages describing what you see and hear. Be sure to make the reader believe he is the one that is over looking the place you're describing.

A local abandoned house is a home for stray animals such as, dogs and field rats. Children in the neighborhood are afraid to play outside due to the stray animals.

Write a letter to your local Mayor asking for his help. Include in the paragraph how the problem can be solved. Remember to include key factors to get the Mayor to help.

Take a camping trip out to the middle of the woods, hike up to a secluded waterfall, or just to your back yard. Be sure to set up your tent and fire pit before dark and get supper and/or s'mores ready.

Before going to sleep write everything that it took for you to get ready to camp, all the way down to finally being able to rest. Include what you are hearing and seeing right now. When you wake up in the morning, be sure to write down everything that you heard over night and all of the morning sounds.

Think of an object, any object will do. Is it round, flat, big or small? Does it have one color or many colors? Can you pick it up and throw it?

Write a paragraph describing your object. Remember to explain what it looks like and what it is made of.

Firemen know how to save people when fires appear. Doctor's helped to heal others in their time of need. Think of someone you know who has been there to help other people deal with crisis.

Write a brief paragraph of eight lines describing what this person does and how they do it.

Pretend you are a young child daydreaming in class. You are dreaming about changing the world for the better. While dreaming, try to come up with several different ideas of how to change the world.

Choose one of your ideas to write about. Write two paragraphs discussing your opinion of this world change.

Think about some great sums of money that you could make from finding a treasure buried on your land. Local historian wants to put the treasure in the city museum without payment while a museum in New York wants to pay greatly for the treasure.

Write a couple of paragraphs expressing your opinion of what is the best way to handle this situation and why you choose it.

Growing up in a flower child community means living closely to others and working to help everyone. Most people have a certain job they do everyday. What would your job be? How will this help the community?

Write an article for a magazine describing your job and the life you live in this flower child community.

You have just received a huge check to re-model a room in your house. What room would you re-model? How do you want to change this room and why? Draw a picture of the room.

Write three paragraphs about this special room, it's remodeling process, and the ending look.

Think of your favorite fairy tale. Create your own fairy tale, using their story as an out-line. Perhaps you are a gnome, a troll, bigger than the forest tree monkeys, or maybe a little red riding wolf.

Write a fairy tale describing your characters and surroundings.

You are a student at the NASCAR College of North Carolina. You are learning many different things about race cars and driving fast on and off the tracks.

Write a letter home telling Mom and Dad about your college and the many different things that you are learning. Describe how your first personal race around the track went.

There are several inventions of communication, known as: the telephone, radio, the computer, and the television. Each one of these inventions has helped people in one way or another. Which of these inventions do you think has helped the greatest number of people?

Write a paragraph giving your opinion of which one is most useful.

Imagine you and your child in a contest of games at your local community fair. What events did you participate in? Did you win or lose? What kind of values did you walk away with? Did you meet new people, share your experiences, or are you just happy to have the privilege of doing something exciting with your child?

Write a one page in your journal explaining your day of fun and games. Include the expressions of your child.

Think about a goal that you have been working on really hard to accomplish. This may involve a sport, hobby, or education, such as: baseball, motor crossing, cross stitching, or writing a poem.

Write a paragraph describing your goal and how you have or will achieved it. Remember to explain in detail what it took or will take to make it happen.

Think about a time when you or someone you know has faced a special predicament. This predicament could be a marriage, the loss of a child, financial difficulties, or maybe even health related.

Write a one page in your journal about this experience. Describe what the predicament is and what was done to resolve this problem.

It's time to refurnish a room in your house. Your mate has given you more than enough money to re-do the walls, floor, and furniture in this room.

Write a brief paragraph describing what the furniture looked like before you make the change. Write a second paragraph why you choose this room to refurnish with the new furniture. On your third paragraph explain what the room looks like now. Draw a diagram of what your room looks like and where each furniture is located, to help you better write your paragraphs.

Pretend you are an archaeologist. You find something never before seen. Draw a picture of your findings.

Write three paragraphs about your findings.
1st paragraph – Describe what your findings look like.
2nd paragraph – Give the finding a name and explain why you gave it this new name.
3rd paragraph – Give conclusions of what you're finding is and what it means to you and the world.

Think about something that is very precious to you. It could be a family member, a pet, or maybe a car or piece of jewelry.

Write two pages in your journal about this precious object or person. Tell what it is and be sure to speak your feelings. Explain why this is so precious to you.

Today you were given a fire safe box to put your valuables in. What objects, documents, pictures, or letters do you have that you would place in the safe for protection? What makes these things so precious and valuable?

Write a list of your valuables.

____________________	____________________
____________________	____________________
____________________	____________________
____________________	____________________

Now write a short story about how you got the safe and why you put your list of valuables in it. Be sure to add where you decided to keep or hide the safe.

Think of something that is memorable to you. It could be a family member, a special vacation, or maybe a flower. What words about this special thing comes to mind?

Write a poem that expresses your thoughts and feelings. Follow the directions for each line of the poem.

The subject (noun)	--- Myrtle Beach
Two Adjectives	--- overrated, crowded
Three verbs	--- sunny, watching, splashing
Four words naming feelings	--- excitement, wonder, break, water
One or two words to replace the subject in the 1st line	--- Fun Vacation

Subject:

Adjectives:

Verbs:

Feelings:

Replacement Subject:

Now write your own poem:

____

____

____

____

Give three words to each of the proper places about the blocked subject.

Nouns

____
____
____

Verbs

____
____
____

Streets Lined of Gold

____
____
____

Adjectives

____
____
____

Words of feelings

Now write a poem or short story about the subject using your words you created.

Use the following Subjects to create more poems and stories using the exact line-up as the above Blocked Subject creation.

Mount Rushmore
Camping on the Parkway
Miniature Dogs
Electrical Illusions
Cross-Country Candidate
A wedding Ceremony
Egyptian Pyramids
Abundance of Love
Niagra Falls
Hurricane Katrina
Bubbling Rapid Rivers
Grand Canyons
Cherokee Indians
Competitive Glory
Majestic Fields of Flowers
Overcoming A Sacrifice
Mummies
Backpacking in the Mountains
Unity of the United States
A Deserted Island

Take the name of the days and months and make a sentence with it. Then write a story using that sentence somewhere within the story.

Sunday *Monday* *Tuesday* *Wednesday*
Thursday *Friday* *Saturday*

January *February* *March* *April*
May *June* *July* *August* *September*
October *November* *December*

Take the name of each day and month and write more words using the letters.

Example:

Sandy
Umbrella
Nasty
Design
Always
Yodel

Now write your own story using those words you created.

____

____

____

____

____

____

Use the following holidays below to begin writing a story. Using only one holiday per story.
By the time you are finished you will have created eight different stories.

New Years Day
Christmas
Valentines Day
Easter

Halloween
Fourth of July
Thanksgiving
Birthdays

Take the following words: sun, moon, and star. Write a story using each word five times or more in your story.

Take the following words: story, truth, and love. Write a story using each word five times or more in your story.

Take the following words: chocolate, cherries, and ice cream. Write a story using each word five times or more in your story.

Take the following words: sand, water, and wind. Write a story using each word five times or more in your story.

Take the following words: cats, mice, and supper. Write a story using each word five times or more in your story.

Take the following words: picture, family, and haunted. Write a story using each word five times or more in your story.

Take the following words: apple pie, cooking, cleaning, chocolate, and pans. Write a story using each word three times or more in your story.

Take the following words: wolves, nighttime, wood, fire, and moon. Write a story using each word three times or more in your story.

Take the following words: TV, radio, telephone, modern, and ages. Write a story using each word three times or more in your story.

Take the following words: missing, abandoned, loved-one, old, and elderly. Write a story using each word three times or more in your story.

Take the following words: chili, bake-off, festival, ice cream, and fun. Write a story using each word three times or more in your story.

Take the following words: summer, wind, winter, snow, and deer's. Write a story using each word three times or more in your story.

Sometimes Scribbling Can Be Fun!

Dylan Jones
2 yrs. old

Sentence Starters for Stories

"I can still see the look on Peter's face when..."

Walking through the deep flower fields of many beautiful colors...

Lou Ann began to crawl at nine months old...

Spike sits on his balcony and plays his flute for everyone to hear. But Lisa down the street thinks...

Tiffany loves to watch her horses run within their fence, until one day she...

Shaybo hums to every song played on the radio. The only thing is...

Lea was cooking down at Mel's Diner while it was being robbed. The heroics she encountered would have made me...

"I am so cold!" cried Tommy. "I know sweetheart," said his Mommy as she cuddled him close in her coat. The weather out here is just to...

Little Timmy was scared. He didn't know if anyone could hear his screams, so he kept yelling, "Help, I'm down here"...

Donnie smacked on his bubble gum. The closer he got to his Dad he began to smack louder. This time his Dad decided that Donnie would...

"These berries will keep us from starving out here," said Lionel, hoping he was right. Karen held her head down and asked, "Lionel, we've been out here for two days. Do you really think anyone is out looking for us yet?"...

Before Johnny could swim back to the boat he was eaten by a great white shark. The blood in the ocean made me...

No one knew what happened to Zack except for me. But there was no way I would ever tell that horrible story. No matter what…

Pulling out the couch we found…

John and I went swimming down by the old barn…

We traveled through the Caribbean's last year on our summer vacation. It has made us want to see more. So this year we are planning a vacation to…

The rose bushes in Mrs. Water's flowerbed are very pretty. I wonder what her secret is…

Our time was almost up. We decided to turn around and go back to the boat. When we did, we saw a…

Little Timmy was triple dogged dared to go inside of the old haunted house down the street. It was scary but Timmy…

Looking for something to do Mary decided to take a walk in the woods. Upon the old gigantic oak tree Mary found…

Monica is taking a course at the local college. She is learning how to cook for David, her new boyfriend. Tonight Monica is preparing her first meal for him…

"Oh no!" exclaimed Dad. "The chicken coop is on fire…"

Piggy always wanted to be King of the Farm. But every time the election would come up Skunky, the reining Stink King always won. Piggy never knew why, but this year he was going to find out…

Nervously I sat in the passenger seat of Casey's car. I tried to wipe the sweat from my hands as my heart pounded to the beat of his speakers. Casey leaned over to me and said, "It will be okay." But my fear of meeting his parents was far to real…

The wild stampeding cattle was coming out of the East. Tex wanted to catch them, so he gathered his things quickly and...

One of Jimmy's morning chores is to feed the horses in the...

The movie we saw last night gave me a nightmare. It seemed so real I didn't...

LaTisha is a fourth grade teacher at Lower Creek. She has several students that can not afford school supplies this year...

Those people living down by the lake have gotten really sick lately...

All the sick children in the hospital received...

When they got to the fair Tony's favorite ride wasn't there...

The Sorbet's won the grand prize in the Cattle Contest, but they didn't place at all in the...

There was an article in the newspaper this morning about the last furniture company in our area. It will be closing down at the end of this month. Now how will we ever survive...

I worked in the kitchen of our small hippie community when I was nine years old. We all shared...

There is a strange man standing by that old building down there. What could he...

"Indians lived off of the earth's land," said the Museum Guide...

Bats flew over head as the lighting struck in the near distance causing all of us to scream with fear...

"Momma, I saw Grandma last night in my room. She was standing at the foot of my bed," cried Joanna. "Honey Grandma lives three hundred miles away form here." Momma barely got the words out when the phone rang…

Johnny ran down the street as happy as could be. He made a sharp turn into Mr. Chow's grocery store and ran straight into him. This caused Johnny to drop his crate of…

Getting off the scales, I wondered, "How in the world did I gain…"

"Search the neighborhood, she has to be around here somewhere," said Aunt Addy…

The statues located in Central Lake Park are truly strangers to our area. Neither one represents Central Lake…

Dana is ecstatic that her mom is going to let her decorate her own bedroom by herself. The only exception is…

Every time Allison goes outside, she starts wheezing really heavily in her chest. Worried about it she goes in and makes…

The pig gobbled up all of Grandma's home made apple pie. The look on her face was priceless…

After working hard all day Terry came home and munched down on some…

The wind howled through the trees. Lisa could only run by the light of the full moon…

The white stallion dragged his injured cowboy down the main street of Dodge Town…

I have been wondering through the endless mountains now for two days. All of a sudden I hear a noise behind me. I take off running North only stopping to take a quick breath. I continued on until I fell…

My friend likes to pretend that she is a doctor. Sometimes...

The dog next door cried loudly all night long. The owners never went to check on him...

The beavers built a dam across the Nocks Lake. It connects the two South openings...

Tara's house is always cozy and warm with a delicate touch of cinnamon aroma running throughout the air...

Her homemade kite was amazing at the show. It is no wonder she won...

His enemies showed great violence in the war against him. Now, how was he going to...

We had to travel by horse to get up to the Hikers Lodge. The hurricane last year caused many trees to fall across the traveling roads. Since then no one has bothered cleaning that part of the mountains up...

The soil here is very rich and good for farming. It is an important resource for...

People used to worship Gods to pray for a good harvest. Now they turn to...

"We will be rich men, " said Nicholas, who could already hear the *tin tin* of the treasure in his dreams. "Yes," said John, "But only if we survive this..."

The lurch of the boat wrenched heavily back and forth as Ann and I held on for dear life. The swill was...

The heat from the sun began to melt the night snow. His boots sloshed through the slush of the early morning...

Clues in the form of fossils of dinosaurs embedded in the rocks have given scientists information about our past. But without ever actually seeing a real dinosaur, some are very...

Falling out of a raft in the middle of an ice-cold river can be frightening. It is even scarier when you realize you are...

Our car broke down in a remote area of the mountains, just a few minutes ago. So Tom decided it was time to...

Jona lifted the sail and pivoted toward the North shoreline. He wanted to...

We went backpacking in the woods of the Blue Ridge Mountains last weekend. We hiked for miles before finding...

She is on the brink of insanity as her friends chose to leave her behind in the woods. "Why would they leave me?" she cried...

Perhaps Lisa's most significant contribution was the money she gave to build the local fire department...

The jury established that Bill was guilty. He was sentenced to...

Grandpa finally went to the eye doctor yesterday and he wasn't very happy when he left. He can see with his new bifocals, but he refuses to...

"I comprehended the fact that you don't love me any more, but you seriously do not have to be rude," said Monica, crying as she drove away...

The founder of our school spoke to the graduates on graduation day. She wanted them to know...

Monster Patty

Caleb Jones
10 yrs. old

Words for Writing

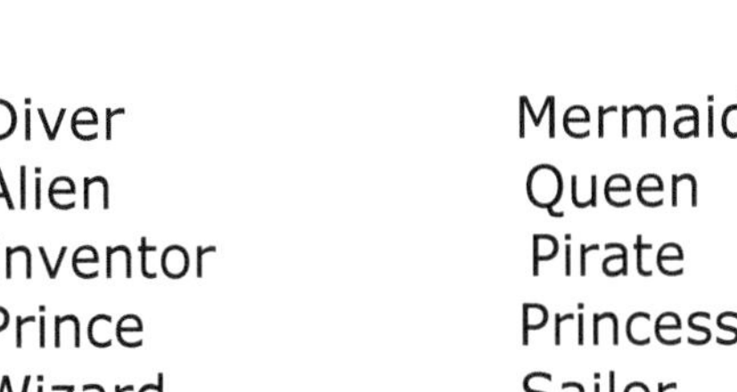

Diver
Alien
Inventor
Prince
Wizard
Knight
Clown
Magician
Mermaid
Queen
Pirate
Princess
Sailor
Fairy
King
Soldier

Ax
Bucket
Ladder
Rope
Lunch Box
Treasure Chest
Camera
Map
Guitar
Cage
Ring
Hammer
Present
Crown
Key
Suitcase

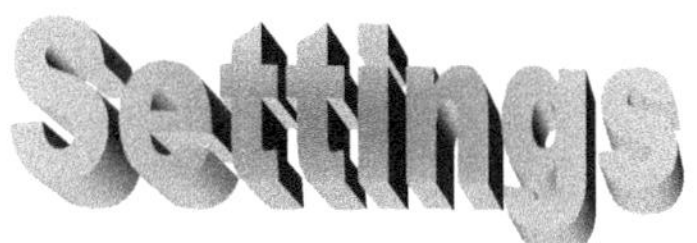

Cliffs
Island
River
Jungle
Swimming Pool
Mountains
Yard
Swamp
Hill
City
Woods
Desert

More Words for Writing

ANGRY

Bad-tempered
Upset
Fed Up
Crabby
Grouchy
Grumpy
Snappy
Annoyed
Irritated
Cross
Fuming
Furious
Livid
Mad

Beautiful

Well-Dressed
Glamorous
Elegant
Sharp
Attractive
Charming
Lovely
Pretty
Graceful
Delightful
Good-looking
Gorgeous
Handsome
Dazzling
Grand
Magnificent
Splendid

ATE or EAT

Chewed
Gnawed
Nibbled
Pecked
Munched
Grazed
Licked
Chomped
Gobble
Guzzled
Pigged
Gorged
Gulped
Snack
Feast
Banquet
Picnic
Barbecue
Breakfast
Brunch
Lunch
Dinner
Supper

Big

Enormous
Huge
Tall
Large
Hefty
Hulking
Colossal
Gigantic
Massive

Bad

Horrible
Horrid
Evil
Nasty
Wicked

Criminal
Sneaky
Rotten
Wicked

Badly-behaved
Disobedient
Mischievous
Naughty
Ill
Sick
Below Par
Unwell
Moldy
Stinking
Stale
Sour

A Bit Of

Piece
Slab
Portion
Slice
Wedge
Chunk
Lump
Morse

Dollop
Mouthful
Scrap
Shred
Fragment
Chip
Crumb
Part

More Words for Writing

Bright

Dazzling
Shiny
Sparkling
Glittering
Gleaming
Colorful
Vivid

Brilliant
Brainy
Sharp
Smart
Clever
Intelligent

Blazing
Glaring
Glowing
Twinkling

Hot

Sizzling
Steaming
Sunny
Scorching
Boiling
Blazing
Baking
Roasting
Bubbling
Scalding
Red – hot
Warm

Noises

Buzz
Meow
Moo
Squeal
Bark
Croak
Growl

Cold

Chilly
Freezing
Frosty
Wintry
Icy
Snowy
Frozen
Shivery

Biting
Bitter
Raw
Stinging

Frightened

Afraid
Terrified
Shocked
Scared
Startled
Fearful
Nervous
Worried
Dismayed
Anxious
Surprised
Astonished

Little

Small
Tiny
Short
Teeny

Baby
Infant
Young

Narrow
Tight

Dirty

Messy
Untidy
Stained
Grubby
Filthy
Greasy
Muddy

Foul
Smoky
Dusty
Grimy

Good

Amazing
Awesome
Fantastic
Thrilling
Incredible
Exciting
Skillful
Talented
Expert
Experienced
Thoughtful
Kind
Caring
Friendly

Enjoyable
Wonderful
Terrific
Fine
Great
Fabulous
Helpful
Polite
Well-behaved
Angelic
Marvelous
Splendid
Excellent
Perfect

Noises

Clap
Snore
Sing
Groan
Wheeze
Burp
Pant
Whistle
Puff
Sniff
Snivel

Ran or Run

Dashed
Speed
Raced
Chased
Bolted
Fled
Rushed
Scrambled
Hurried
Jogged
Sprinted

Beautifully Landscaped

Isaac Jones
8 yrs. old

Logical Acquaintances

Common words that help show logical connections between sentences or between ideas.

- Additional facts – again, another, also, and besides, further, furthermore, finally, in conclusion, initially, next to begin with
- Cause – because, since, for this reason
- Contrasts – although, but, despite, either, however, in ,if, even though, spite of, neither, still, unless, instead, yet
- Emphasis – basically, certainly, of course, in fact, indeed, essentially
- Place – above, among, below, beyond, nearby, adjacent, farther, opposite, there, under
- Result – as a result, for this reason, obviously, so, consequently, therefore
- Similarities – as, as though, also, in the same way, like, similarly
- Specific examples – especially, for example, specifically, particular

If the verb is irregular, be careful to choose the correct form.

Verb	**Past**	
Become	Became	has become
Begin	Began	has begun
Blow	Blew	has blown
Bring	Brought	has brought
Buy	Bought	has bought
Catch	Caught	has caught
Choose	Chose	has chosen
Do	Did	has done
Eat	Ate	has eaten
Fly	Flew	has flown
Give	Gave	has given
Go	Went	has gone
Grow	Grew	has grown
Have, has	Had	has had
Hit	Hit	has hit
Know	Knew	has known
Leave	Left	has left
Let	Let	has let
Mean	Meant	has meant
Ride	Rode	has ridden
Run	Ran	has run
See	Saw	has seen
Sing	Sang	has sung
Strike	Struck	has struck
Take	Took	has taken
Tell	Told	has told
Think	Thought	has thought
Write	Wrote	has written

Imagination is what gets us motivated

Kathy Jones
37 yrs. old

Fun time with words

Fill in the blanks with your own chosen words.
Be creative make us laugh, cry, sad, or happy.

_____________ hears his name. "_______________, do you want to play?" asks a group of pee wee _________________players. "Why not?" he says. He changes into his _____________ uniform and joins the kids on the _____________ field. "Lets play ________!" It is ______________ turn at the ball. _____________! Whoa, look at that ball go! The ball is heading out of the _____________. The kids love what they ___________. "Thank you for letting me join in on the __________!" says ____________, as he waves goodbye.

Casey's friends are ______________ and ________________. He feels ____________ when they are _____________. Each one's special in their own _____________. Casey _____________ them more each __________. He thinks _______________ can really _____________ fast. He always makes it look ______________! Casey thinks ____________ is really _____________. She can read a _________ and know it by ___________. Casey also thinks _____________ paints with __________. Her latest ________________ is sure to ________________. "I ________ my friends and all ___________ ____________. I guess that means I like me, too."

Many animals live on the _____________. The __________ and her ________ live in the ____________. The ____________ and the __________ live in the ____________. Mama _______ and her ____________ live in a house called a _____________. Mama _________- and the ____________ live near the __________. They love to ____________ and _____________! This home is called a _____________. All the ____________ and their ____________ love to romp in the __________. They also like to eat the _____________ that grows _____________. The _________ and the ___________ are birds that live mostly on the _____________. They share the little ___________ that's on the ________. The ____________ hutch is the ___________ home. It's where they keep their ______________.

Ms. Cannon was a favorite _____________ at the ___________ Institute for _____________ Learning. The students thought she was _____________ but always ____________. The students also ___________ to see Ms. Cannon use her ____________ powers. As _________, she could change the _______________ to do whatever she wanted. As her _________ began to _______________, she would raise her _____________ in the _____________ and summon ______________. She only used her _________ powers to _________ the ____________ in their fight to _____________ the ____________. There were some ________ mutants who believed that humans and mutants couldn't __________________ together. They wanted to ____________ the humans and take over the ______________. Together with the rest of the _________, ___________ would fight the ____________ mutants to keep the ________________ safe. The next time you see ___________ in the _____________, it could be that ________________ is coming!

__________ and __________ are best friends. They do everything together. They __________ their __________ in the __________. They play __________. At home they help each other __________ leaves. They play __________ on the __________. One day it __________ and __________ called __________ on the phone. "Let's build a __________," he said. The __________ is very __________ and __________, but they are having a __________ time. The next day they __________ to school. There was a new __________ at their school. His name is __________. __________ is very __________. He put __________ on __________ chair. He pushed __________ on the __________. __________ and __________ did not like __________ at all. After school, __________ and __________ built another __________. Then they saw __________. He said, "This __________ stinks." __________ yelled, "Don't get our __________ mad. He's __________ and he will __________ you!" __________ just __________. That night __________ and __________ made up a plan to get even with __________ __________. They were going to really __________ him. They got a __________ and turned it on. They made __________ noises. Then they took the __________ __________ outside. They hid behind their __________ they built and waited for __________ __________ to come by. __________ came down the sidewalk. They turned on the __________ __________. "WAAAAA!" screamed the __________. "He's alive!" __________ cried. He __________ and __________ behind a __________. __________ and __________ laughed so hard that they __________ on the ground. __________ saw __________ and __________ laughing. "That was __________," he said. "I never met a talking __________ before." "He just __________ here," said __________. Then they all began to laugh together.

Long ago, there were three ____________. There was __________ the __________. There was _______ the __________. And there was ________ the ___________. One night, ___________ said, "I am a ___________." "I will go for a _____________." She ____________ on her special _______________. Up, up, up, went ____________. High in the ________ went __________ the ____________. One night, the second ____________ said, "I am a ____________." "I will go for a ___________." She ___________ on her special __________. Up, up, up, went ____________. ___________ in the _________ went ___________ the ____________. One night, the third _____________, ____________ said, "I am a ____________." "I want to go for a _____________." "But I do not have a special ________." "I do not have a special ___________." "How will I go for a _____________?" said ___________ the _________. "WE will go for a _____________," said the __________ bird. "__________ on my back. We will go for a ____________." She ___________ on the ____________ bird's back. High in the ___________ went ____________ and the ___________ bird. Up in the___________ went ___________ and ____________ and _______________.

Is everyone ready? It's time to _____________ a ____________! _____________ your _____________! _____________ your ____________. Waggle your ______________ and wiggle your _____________. __________ your ____________ and jiggle your ____________. Flap your ______________. ______________ your shoulders. ___________ your arms. Touch your ______________. _____________ up your ___________ and make a ______________. _____________ your waist. Now __________ your ____________ and wave _____________.

One happy ________________. Two _____________ teachers. Three _____________ towers made by four ____________ builders. Five ____________ and ________________. _____________ good listeners. Seven great ________________ using eight different ____________. Nine pairs of ______________, eating ten _________________ apples. Nine high __________ over eight hide and ____________. Seven ___________ sleepers. Six in a hurry to use the _______________! Five _________ projects. ____________ busy workers. Three ____________ cages. Two stuck ____________. One happy ____________.

Last month, I went ____________ with Mommy and Daddy. I found some new playmates--- two baby ____________. I was having so much _______________ that I didn't see Mama ____________. She didn't want ______________ playing with her babies. She ___________ at me. I was in deep ______________. Then I heard a _____________ ___________. Guess who was ______________! Mama ___________ was _______________ when she saw my _____________ dog. She ________ even forgetting her babies. I told my _____________ dog that Mama __________ was only protecting her babies. My good ___________ dog took the baby ____________ back to Mama _____________. Then he took us all back to ___________.

One night Little _____________ said, "I will _______ on my __________." He ___________ very ________. "No, no Little ________," said his __________. "It is not ___________ to play that way." But Little ___________ went on ___________. He __________ higher and higher until he _____________ off the _____________ and __________ on the ___________. Mama ___________ picked him up. "No, no, Little ____________," she said. "____________ are not for ____________. ____________ are for ____________." She _________ the bump on his ____________ and tucked Little __________ safely in __________.

Sarah ____________ a friend. "Hi, Sarah," said her friend. "Let's __________ our ________." "I can __________ very __________," said Sarah. She ____________ on her ___________ and went very fast down the ___________. "No," yelled her friend. "It is not ________ to ____________ that way." But Sarah went ___________ and ________ down the ___________. She went so ___________ she took a ____________.

When it is __________ outside, Donnie puts on his __________. He puts on his ____________ and his ____________. He puts his ________ on his _________ and __________ on his hands. He wears a lot of _____________ when it's _________ outside. The ___________ keep him ___________ while she builds a _____________.

Words out of Words

How many words can you make from the following words?

Example:

Stage Coach

Cage	Ache
Toga	Chose
Gate	Sage

Accommodation

Intermediary

Descendants

Illumination

Environment

Vegetation

Undergrowth

Rehearsal

Amusement

Congregation

Compassionate

Despicable

Incorporation

Responsibility

Establishment

Characteristic

Undergrowth

Rehearsal

Interruption

Multitude

Sympathetic

Horrendous

Fascination

Accountability

Organization

Diplomatic

Undergrowth

Rehearsal

Cheerfulness

Avoidance

Appreciative

Outrageous

Hodgepodge

Rendezvous

Emancipation

Authorization

This exercise will teach you to look at a word a little differently. Take one word, such as Costumes and divide that word into four more words that are related. You can use the examples below or make up your own words to each topic. Then begin a story using each word. You should have four different stories created by the time you are finished with one topic.

Topic:
Costumes

Halloween, Party, Festival, Theater

Crops

Vegetables, Spices, Fruit, Trees-Flowers

Clothes

Costumes, Home-Made, Tank-Top, Sweater

Children

Babies, Sisters, Brothers, Neighbors

Symbols

Musical, Road-Signs, Numbers, Games

Spring

Season, Coil, Watering Hole, Cool

Decorations

Party, Elections, Birthday, Showers

Ruler

President, King, Teacher, Priest

Exercise

Walking, Hiking, Water Skiing, Bicycle

Tractor

Transfer, Garden, Construction, Toys

Existence

Life, Reality, Survival, Endurance

Clock

Timepiece, Grandfather, Device, Face

Animal

Monster, Creature, Being, Wild

Mask

Camouflage, Cover, Surgical, Veil

Love

Adore, Worship, Passion, Sweetheart

Grass

Medical, Pasture, Prairie, Meadow

Light

Stars, Sun, Radiance, Glow

Creative Thinking

Use the words below to write a sentence.

Afterwards go back and find the sentences you like best and use them as story starters.

Humor	Strawberries	Elephant	Glasses	Fire
Talent	Banana	Rabbit	Eyes	Test
Career	Lemon	Rug	Campfire	Jogger
Studio	Fiber	Towels	Pencil	Expert
Character	Grain	Hanger	Adventure	Mold
Entertainment	World	Curtain	Scary	Grass
Squeezed	Hand	Soap	Imaginary	Trees
Custom	Pray	Dish	Tents	Penicillin
Brilliant	Kneel	Spoon	Business	Spring
Simply	Church	Cup	Partner	Wreck
Transform	Preacher	Pans	Store	Crew
Beauty	Turtle	Stove	Sales	Fireman
Heart	Gnat	Book	Buyers	Cats
Sweet	Horse	Paper	Energy	Truck

Chant	Master	Gasp	Jesting
Sing	Dancer	Fossil	Genius
Festival	Bail	Wonder	Profession
Elders	Career	Think	Bungalow
Ancestor	Audience	Love	Atmosphere
Skull	Costume	Adore	Distraction
Horror	Arrange	Observe	Harass
Leather	Vast	Believe	Habit
Mask	Sparkle	Relic	Accomplished
Storyteller	Thick	Childhood	Modestly
Graceful	Tuxedo	Remnant	Convert
Laughter	Orchard	Remains	Splendor
Muscle	Lizard	Existence	Spirit
Melody	Famous	Legendary	Obliging

Word Search
to inspire your imagination

C	R	E	A	T	E	Z	S	U	T
J	O	M	A	E	R	D	G	O	P
K	I	N	V	E	N	T	U	M	P
N	B	E	S	H	A	C	T	B	I
O	E	D	C	T	H	L	F	U	C
I	L	V	K	H	R	K	A	I	T
H	I	G	M	I	S	U	R	L	U
S	E	S	I	N	F	O	C	D	R
A	V	U	R	K	C	L	D	T	E
F	E	I	M	A	G	I	N	E	D

Touch	Picture	Imagine	Think	Create	Dream
Believe	Craft	Build	Fashion	Construct	Invent

Q	M	S	Q	U	I	R	R	E	L
R	G	X	B	F	H	A	S	A	W
E	D	O	V	K	L	E	P	G	O
G	A	W	H	E	Y	B	G	L	D
I	S	P	I	D	E	R	S	E	X
T	N	Q	V	C	N	F	P	T	J
R	A	M	J	Y	R	U	A	G	B
U	K	X	O	F	S	N	O	I	L
D	E	E	R	X	B	L	D	R	H
O	C	P	A	N	T	H	E	R	G

Tiger	Lion	Bear	Snake	Groundhog	Squirrel
Panther	Owl	Deer	Fox	Spiders	Eagle

N	A	I	C	I	S	U	M	D	Y
K	L	B	N	W	P	C	C	T	C
S	M	A	H	R	A	R	S	N	O
S	I	J	M	G	I	I	C	A	M
C	X	N	E	R	N	T	U	T	E
W	A	I	G	M	T	I	L	S	D
S	C	C	U	E	E	C	P	I	I
K	T	L	T	I	R	W	T	T	A
C	O	M	E	D	I	A	O	R	N
C	R	W	R	I	T	E	R	A	S

Comedian **Sculptor** **Writer** **Painter** **Critic**

Singer **Actor** **Artist** **Musician** **Columnist**

K	R	O	W	E	M	O	H	B	G
O	O	W	H	O	M	R	G	A	N
O	K	E	U	L	G	E	B	G	O
B	P	R	P	E	R	K	G	L	Y
E	A	A	S	S	O	R	S	U	A
T	P	S	N	O	P	A	P	E	R
O	E	E	B	W	E	M	O	H	C
N	P	R	D	F	O	L	D	E	R
T	E	S	C	I	S	S	O	R	S
P	M	C	L	I	C	N	E	P	M

Pencil **Pens** **Paper** **Notebook** **Erasers** **Marker**

Crayon **Folder** **Bookbag** **Homework** **Glue** **Scissor**

S	E	D	O	S	I	P	E	C	A
L	D	I	A	R	Y	A	G	H	M
I	S	Y	L	I	F	P	B	A	O
F	T	R	A	I	D	E	G	P	V
I	N	O	V	E	L	A	Z	T	I
L	O	T	R	A	Z	A	G	E	E
M	R	S	E	I	R	E	S	R	S
S	L	A	N	R	U	O	J	O	U
E	Y	E	L	C	I	T	R	A	R
P	E	R	I	O	D	I	C	A	L

Movies **Magazine** **Series** **Novel** **Episodes** **Journal**

Periodical **Article** **Story** **Chapter** **Diary** **Films**

M	T	E	R	E	H	P	S	Q	R
E	L	G	N	A	T	C	E	R	C
S	L	E	C	E	N	G	L	H	L
Q	G	R	A	B	U	Q	S	O	E
U	N	S	Q	U	A	R	E	M	L
A	A	B	E	C	U	M	E	B	C
D	I	A	M	O	N	D	I	U	R
T	R	I	A	N	G	L	E	S	I
F	T	E	T	R	A	G	O	N	C
I	G	E	R	U	G	I	F	I	G

Square **Circle** **Rectangle** **Diamond** **Triangle**

Cube **Sphere** **Rhombus** **Figure** **Tetragon**

Sheriff
Better hold your guns!
Ethan Jones
4 yrs. old

Fill In's For Fun

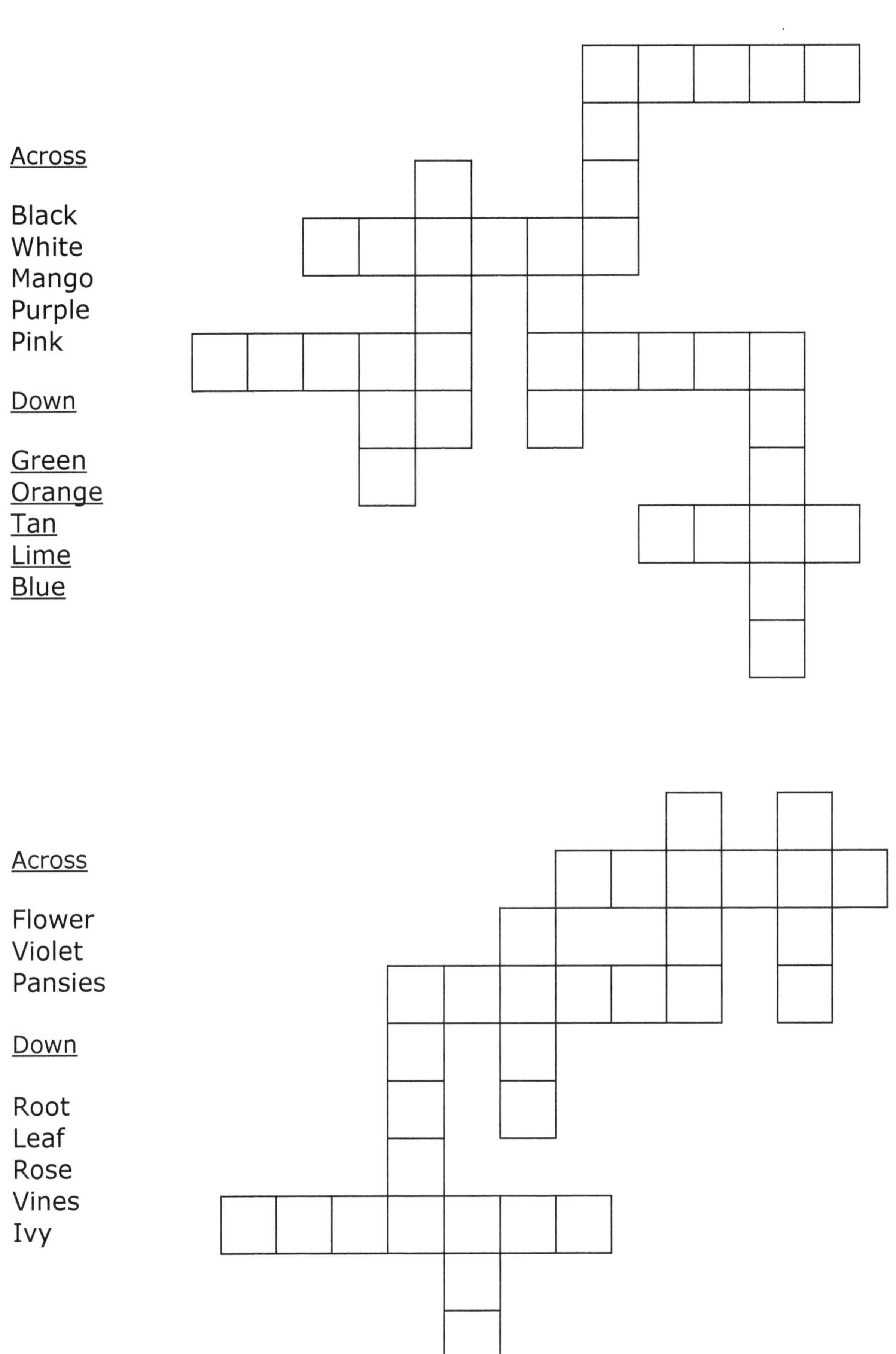

Across

Black
White
Mango
Purple
Pink

Down

Green
Orange
Tan
Lime
Blue

Across

Flower
Violet
Pansies

Down

Root
Leaf
Rose
Vines
Ivy

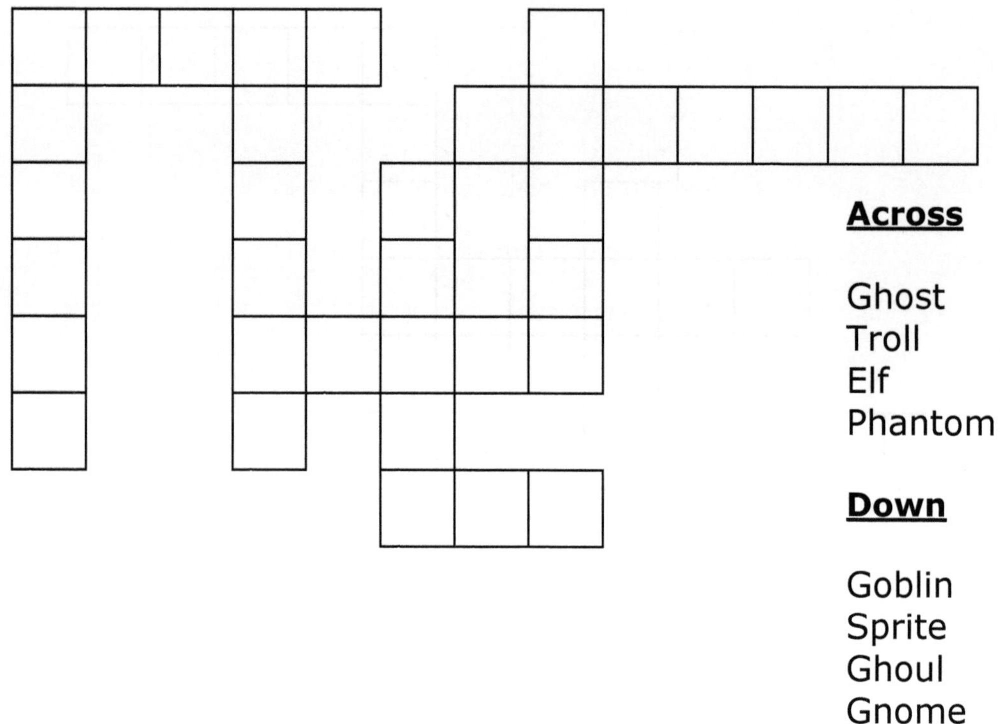

Across

Ghost
Troll
Elf
Phantom

Down

Goblin
Sprite
Ghoul
Gnome

Across

Weddings
Groom
Attached
Connubial

Down

Cake
Dress
Conjugal
Bridal

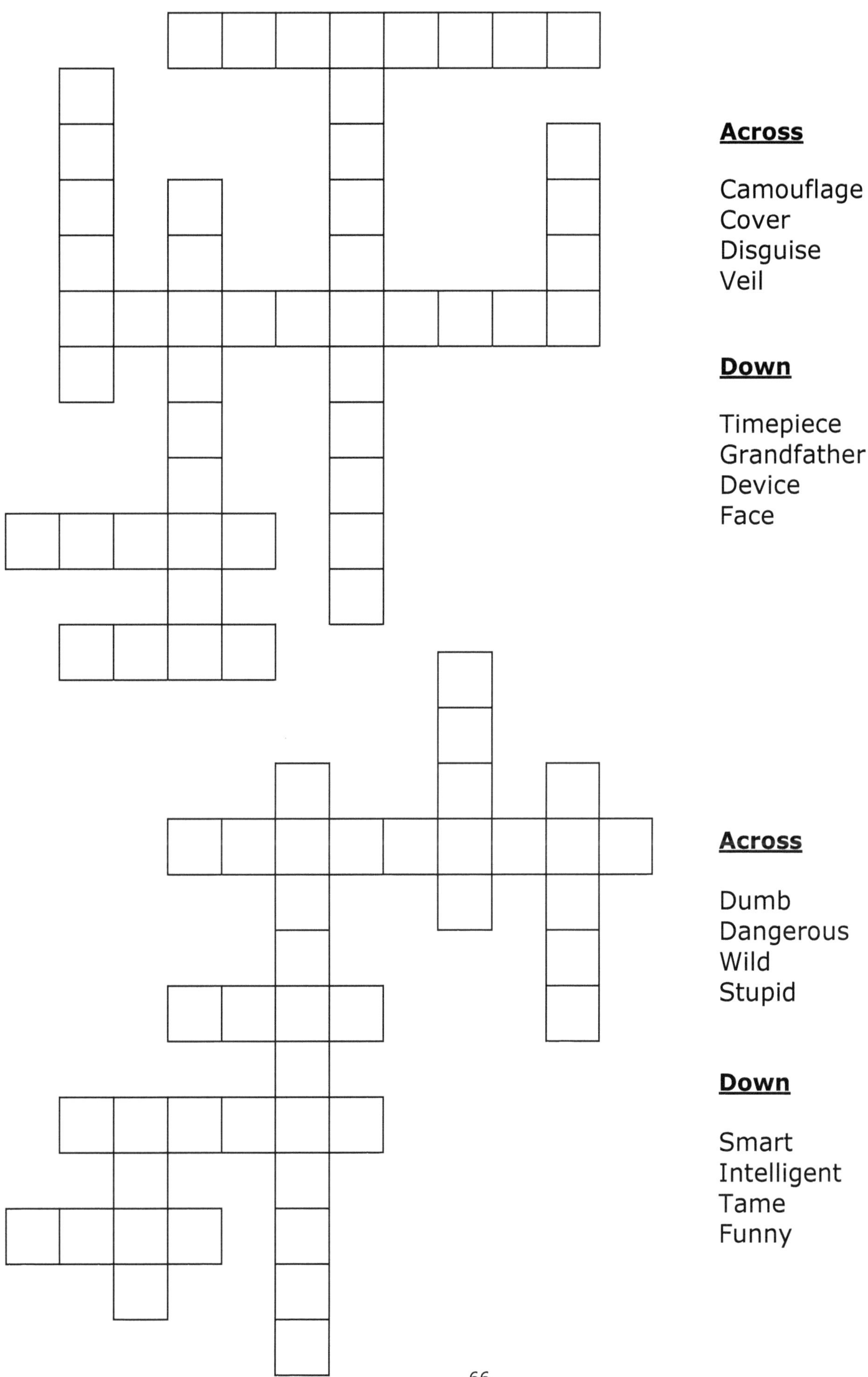

Across

Camouflage
Cover
Disguise
Veil

Down

Timepiece
Grandfather
Device
Face

Across

Dumb
Dangerous
Wild
Stupid

Down

Smart
Intelligent
Tame
Funny

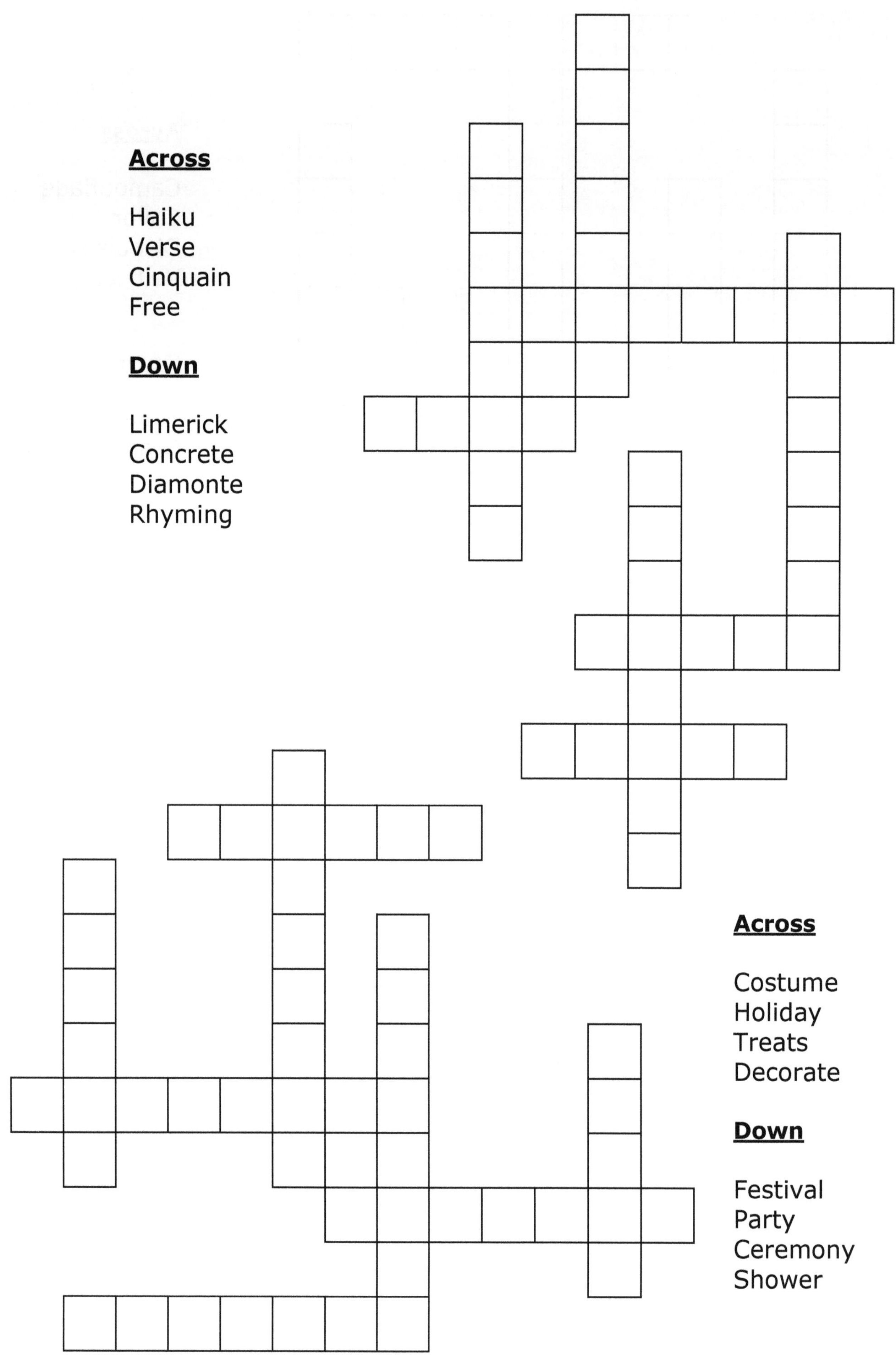
Across
Haiku
Verse
Cinquain
Free
Down
Limerick
Concrete
Diamonte
Rhyming
Across
Costume
Holiday
Treats
Decorate
Down
Festival
Party
Ceremony
Shower

Unscrambling the Words

Then use each word twice in a short story

(This exercise will teach you to write an interesting story using descriptive words correctly, but remember not so sound repetitive when using your words below.)

Renovating Earth

Mronvtieen ______________________________

Tmpopcs ______________________________

Cigecnyrl ______________________________

Spatnl ______________________________

Rtsha ______________________________

Lupidont ______________________________

Vrrpeniote ______________________________

Tetlri ______________________________

Enviroment, Compost, Recycling, Plants, Trash, Pollution, Prevention, Litter

Smart Heart

Gbelegevsta ______________________________

Yhhetal ______________________________

Riftus ______________________________

Sntu ______________________________

Daireyt ______________________________

Ichcseo ______________________________

Dagern ______________________________

Adsla ______________________________

Vegetables, Healthy, Fruits, Nuts, Dietary, Choices, Garden, Salad

Unscrambling the Words
Then use each word twice in a short story

Plotting Words

spwaepenr ______________________

sreecsrou ______________________

qpmutneie ______________________

abyirl ______________________

gazaimne ______________________

rceserah ______________________

cniofit ______________________

fnionntico ______________________

Newspaper, Resources, Equipment, Libary, Magazine, Research, Fiction, Nonfiction

Mountain Outburst

mcupei ______________________

ovonalc ______________________

isndpxoe ______________________

tunirope ______________________

souregan ______________________

hlupurusos ______________________

koesm ______________________

pluavhae ______________________

Upheaval, Volcano, Explosion, Eruption, Dangerous, Sulphurous, Smoke, Pumice

Unscrambling the Words
Then use each word twice in a short story

Plotting Words

spwaepenr ______________________________

sreecsrou ______________________________

qpmutneie ______________________________

abyirl ______________________________

gazaimne ______________________________

rceserah ______________________________

cniofit ______________________________

fnionntico ______________________________

Newspaper, Resources, Equipment, Libary, Magazine, Research, Fiction, Nonfiction

Mountain Outburst

mcupei ______________________________

ovonalc ______________________________

isndpxoe ______________________________

tunirope ______________________________

souregan ______________________________

hlupurusos ______________________________

koesm ______________________________

pluavhae ______________________________

Upheaval, Volcano, Explosion, Eruption, Dangerous, Suplhurous, Smoke, Pumice

Unscrambling the Words
Then use each word twice in a short story

Production Time

nipogsmi ____________________

actcharers ____________________

rogutifiev ____________________

tcureaer ____________________

nudetri ____________________

lltisutare ____________________

fopremracne ____________________

cedomy ____________________

degraty ____________________

teathre ____________________

Imposing, Characters, Figurative, Creature, Intrude, Illustrate, Performance, Comedy, Tragedy, Theater

Amorous Love

sapsateion ____________________

slozeua ____________________

criotamn ____________________

dideddtace ____________________

tatefuani ____________________

westearhet ____________________

ledovbe ____________________

georguos ____________________

leledecatb ____________________

diav ____________________

Passionate, Zealous, Romantic, Dedicated, Infatuate, Sweetheart, Beloved, Gorgeous, Delectable, Avid

Unscrambling the Words
Then use each word three times in a short story

Retreat Fun

sihf ____________________

kieh ____________________

miws ____________________

hntu ____________________

pcam ____________________

Fish, Hike, Swim, Hunt, Camp

Exhilarating Joy

tirb bkie ____________________

Ksy vied ____________________

Cork bimlc ____________________

Ninksy pdi ____________________

Adns frus ____________________

Dirt bike, Sky dive, Rock climb, Skinny dip, Sand surf

Shifty Aid

vermanue ____________________

opocarteino ____________________

hechme ____________________

lobaloctanio ____________________

otpieoran ____________________

Maneuver, Cooperation, Scheme, Collaboration, Operation

Guru

vidoasr ____________________

goculelae ____________________

rsopsofr ____________________

turlecer ____________________

tcnoantsul ____________________

Advisor, Colleague, Professor, Lecturer, Consultant

Visual Aid

Tavetiegon ____________________

loifaeg ____________________

buerbrhys ____________________

rolaf ____________________

howdorubs ____________________

Vegetation, Foliage, Shrubbery, Flora, Brushwood

Backyard Greenery

dodloe ____________________

qguigels ____________________

warignd ____________________

ticurpe ____________________

tonaorc ____________________

Doodle, Squiggle, Drawing, Picture, Cartoon

Truckin Down Spider Lane

Elijah Erwood
12 yrs. old

Nouns

Nouns are naming words for people, animals, things, and places.

Pronouns

Pronoun is a word like I, or me, or she, or his, or they.
Pronouns have different forms.
When it is the subject of a sentence, it will have one of these: I, you, he, she, it, we, or they.
When the pronoun comes after a verb or a preposition (like to, for, with, about, or between) it will have one of these: me, you, it, her, us, or them.
When a pronoun is used to show possession or ownership, it will have one of these: my, mine, your, yours, his, her, its our ours, their, or theirs.

Adjectives

Adjectives describe or tell about nouns or pronouns.

Verbs

Verbs are doing words. They tell you what is happening in a sentence.

Adverbs

Adverbs describe or tell about verbs, adjectives, or other adverbs.

Connective

Connectives are also called, joining words. You can make a sentence longer and more interesting by using a connective.

Subject-Verb Agreement

The form of a verb depends on two things:

- Whether the subject of the sentence is singular or plural.
- Whether the verb shows an action in the present or the past tense.

The present tense of a verb ends in –s or –es when the subject is a singular noun or one of these pronouns: he, she, and it.

The present tense of the verb does NOT have an –s or an –es ending added to it when the subject is a plural noun or one of these pronouns: I, we, you, and they.

A compound subject is like a plural subject. The present tense of the verb does not have –s or –es added to it.

The verb be is special. It has different forms in both the present tense and the past tense.

Capitalization

Capitalize the first word in a sentence.
Capitalize the pronoun I wherever it appears.
Capitalize a title used before a person's last name.
Capitalize each important word in the title of a written work.
Capitalize the first word in a direct quotation
Capitalize proper nouns.

Punctuation

Use a period at the end of a statement or a command.
Use a period at the end of an abbreviation.
Use a question mark at the end of a question.
Use an exclamation point at the end of a sentence that shows strong feeling.

Commas

Use a comma between words in a series of three or more things.
Use a comma before a direct quotation.
Use a comma between the day and year in a date.
Use a comma between city and state.
Use a comma after the opening of a friendly letter.
Use a comma after the closing of a letter.

Apostrophes

Use an apostrophe in possessives.
Use an apostrophe in contractions.

Other Books from the Author Kathy Scruggs Erwood Georgina Jones

Andy LoStone Adventures in Kill Devil Hills

Andy and his friend Nick go to spend the summer with Andy's Aunt Tawnie. Once there, they begin to hear cries, screams and things that go bump in the night. Andy decides that it is time to find out what is going on.
www.publishamerica.com

Stepping Stones of War

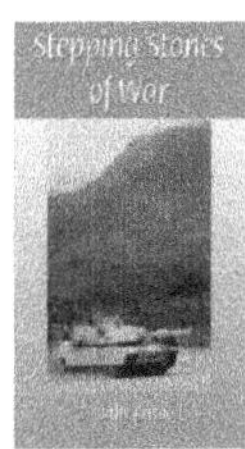

The rolling roar of military tanks – screaming people scurrying in the streets – the cries of panic - stricken children – all the *Stepping Stones of War*.
www.publishamerica.com

The Mesner House

Andy, being one that loves an adventure wants to go inside of Old Man Mesner's house to see how an old callous man lived. Rumors have floated around town that he was a very mean and nasty man who ran off his wife in a beating rage; other rumors say that Old Man Mesner killed his wife and two children before becoming a miser of loneliness.
www.lulu.com

Our Daily Bread Diabetic Cookbook

What is this thing they call Diabetes? Why does it control our Bodies? What does it have to do with what we eat? Learning to recognize the symptoms of diabetes is an important way to detect the condition early. Our Daily Bread Diabetic Cookbook will show you how to control your diabetes and what you can eat with a great taste and flavor of delicious foods.
www.lulu.com

www.ingramcontent.com/pod-product-compliance
Ingram Content Group UK Ltd.
Pitfield, Milton Keynes, MK11 3LW, UK
UKHW051136260726
13967UKWH00010B/3094

9 781257 089215